IMAGES
of America

SKYTOP LODGE

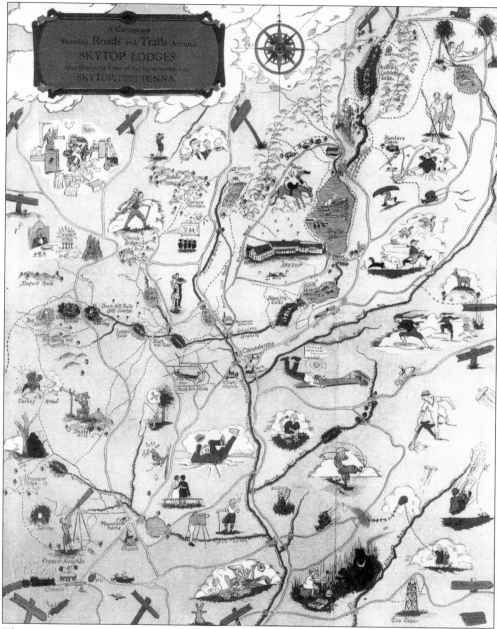

This 1940s map, "Cartograph Showing Roads and Trails Around Skytop Lodges," playfully illustrates recreational activities surrounding Skytop in Monroe County, Pennsylvania. A puzzle version of this map was sold as a novelty. (Courtesy of Lucille May and Kendric Packer.)

ON THE COVER: Early morning breakfast rides were popular for many years at Skytop. A riding master would lead groups from the stables to the trout stream trail and head out toward Goose Pond. Riders would climb up Skytop Mountain to find Skytop chefs cooking breakfast over an open fire. The highlight of the four-hour ride was the stunning 270-degree vista that included the Delaware Water Gap and Skytop Lodge. (Courtesy of the Skytop Lodge Archives.)

IMAGES
of America

SKYTOP LODGE

Claire Gierwatowski
on behalf of Skytop Lodge

ARCADIA
PUBLISHING

Published by Arcadia Publishing
Charleston, South Carolina

Printed in the United States of America

Library of Congress Control Number: 2014954871

For all general information, please contact Arcadia Publishing:
Telephone 843-853-2070
Fax 843-853-0044
E-mail sales@arcadiapublishing.com
For customer service and orders:
Toll-Free 1-888-313-2665

Visit us on the Internet at www.arcadiapublishing.com

This book is dedicated to the memory of Samuel H. Packer.

CONTENTS

ACKNOWLEDGMENTS

Skytop's current president and general manager, Douglas Hustad, has prioritized not only preserving Skytop's history, but also communicating that history to Skytop guests and future guests. For that mission, I am grateful, and I would like to thank Arcadia Publishing for providing the perfect vehicle to accomplish that mission—the Images of America series. I feel very fortunate to have been a part of this project. My thanks to Carol Gallopo for putting me in the right spot at the right time.

Just under half of the images used in this book have come from outside sources. Any not credited as such have come from Skytop's own archive collection. I had the great pleasure of meeting Lucille May and Kendric Packer after spending several months researching their father, Samuel Packer. Their wonderful contributions added immeasurably to this book, and their friendship has become invaluable to me personally. Another significant resource was given by the family of Barclay White. To Jim White and Margaret White Winters, I am grateful for the images and your prompt responses to my endless emails. Thank you also to Eve Myers Doherty, who contributed beautiful scrapbooks and other materials about Skytop and likewise suffered many questions.

Skytop has touched many people's lives over the years. Gratefully, those that I reached out to were kind enough to share their Skytop story with me. Acknowledgments and thanks must be given to Richard Price, Tim Smith, Lynne Derby Graham, Holly Augenbach, Leigh Berrien, Thomas Skeans, Keith Cambell, June McHugh, Paul and Jean Gravel, Richard Krummell, Barry Sommers, Michelle Lanoir, Andrea Battern, Danielle Rake, Connie Perrill, Bob Baldassari, Gene Yakubowski, Claudia and William Malleson, Nancy Hudock, Eleanor Biles, Ed Mayotte, and Doug Smith. Each person added to or preserved Skytop's story in some way. My apologies to those whose names I have forgotten.

To Joanne Seese, Leeanne Dyson, and Nell Boucher, thank you for providing time and images from your respective archives, the Barrett Township Historical Society and Mohonk Mountain House Archives. To Eric Woodward, thank you for holding onto your grandfather's drawings of Skytop Lodge. And to Teresa McNamara, Lawrence Squeri, and Nicolette Witcher, thank you for sacrificing your own limited time to offer encouragement, support, and editorial assistance.

To my family, Greg, Rayvin, and Dylan, thank you.

INTRODUCTION

All this Skytop land had to be cleared first of tall trees-then the task of clearing the land of stones, stones and stones. Oxen and a stone boat carried them to many stone walls. The whole family would help the picking and loading of the stones; -little girls, boys, mama and papa. These stones from the stone walls Skytop used to build this fine building. What a monument to the early settlers indeed- and what a fine place many of their heirs may come to enjoy the good things in life.

—Edna Palmer Engelhardt, 1971

The land features, climate, and ecology of the Poconos are owed to the geology that placed the Pocono escarpment right through the middle of Monroe County and Skytop property. The edge of the escarpment is clearly visible and parts of it have been named—Mount Wismer, West Mountain, and Skytop Mountain. Now that the spruces and pines have grown tall on the once-plowed plateau, one must climb these high edges to view the panoramic gaps and valleys to the south. It is these high edges over which the waters of the Leavitt Branch tumble, not once, but twice, forming two of the most scenic and special waterfalls in the Poconos.

The highest point of the Poconos is slightly over 2,000 feet. In the early 1900s, industrialization had the dual effect of creating both wealth and pollution. To those who could afford to escape the pollution, those 2,000 feet were mountainous compared to the coastal city centers of New York and Philadelphia, Pennsylvania. "Skytop Lodge—High in the Poconos" was the slogan that was shouted out as often and in as many ways as possible. From before the lodge opened its doors until the late 1960s, promotions of the resort leaned heavily on the idea that vacationers would feel as if they were on top of the world.

One of the first questions guests ask when they arrive at Skytop Lodge is, "Was this place always a hotel?" Unlike many other historic hotels, Skytop has been a continuously operating hotel from its opening in 1928 to the present day. No fires, world wars, or economic downturns have caused its doors to close. Skytop has tenaciously navigated the currents of the hotel industry through changes in transportation, technology, and economy, striving constantly to balance its traditions with new trends.

A second question on the lips of any new Skytopper is, "Who owns Skytop?" The answer to this makes for an interesting tale. No single endowment or inheritance made Skytop possible. It was a dream, nourished by a very few, that grew through the tireless work of many. Developed under the auspices of two different companies formed in 1925, the original companies incorporated were the operating company, Sky Top Lodges, Inc., and the parent company, Pocono Hotels Corporation. Stock in the parent company, Pocono Hotels Corporation, was sold to finance the construction of Skytop Lodge.

Skytop was very much a speculative investment conceived during the heyday of economic growth that followed World War I. All the prosperity, hope, and technical advances of 1920s America coalesced in a small group of people who made Skytop Lodge possible. There were key investors in the project, but most of the capital used was borrowed. Not one, but two mortgages financed the $1 million building. The first mortgage was backed by the property, and the second was secured with bonds put up at the last minute by two Atlantic City, New Jersey, hoteliers. Still, it was not enough. A third financial instrument was created—gold notes. Mostly purchased by people who were already stockholders, these gold notes raised the final monies needed for the project. Not a single person alive could have anticipated the financial crash that occurred just a year after the lodge opened for business. It took four separate extensions and 20 years for those notes to be paid. That Skytop has remained open when other, older establishments have failed is a testament to Skytop Lodge and the people who have run it. The speculation paid off. And if memories count, it paid off in dividends.

The story goes that Skytop came about because some patrons of the Quaker resort Buck Hill Falls wanted a resort that was less restrictive. Philadelphia Quakers had founded Buck Hill in 1901 and practiced behavior and decorum that followed Quaker philosophies. Card playing and dancing, for example, were prohibited. Another Quaker resort, Pocono Manor, opened in 1902 and operated in a similar fashion. Two decades later, the Jazz Age was in full swing. When Skytop opened in 1928, three miles north of Buck Hill, music and dancing were featured activities and two card rooms were built to accommodate bridge players.

A copy of a somewhat risqué Buck Hill cheer exemplifies the perceived difference between the resorts. Called "Beulah Land," a chorus of "Yea, morals matter" is followed by these lyrics:

On First Day eve, we picnic high
On Sky Top Mountain 'neath the sky;
Though they drink beer in the woods
The Buck Hill girls don't deliver the goods.

At Sky Top they all live in sin;
We live the good life at the Inn
Trim our morals, never loose,
Hail thou chaste tomato juice.

After Prohibition ended in 1933, while the two Quaker resorts remained dry, Skytop installed a bar and began wine service in the dining room. Whether or not Skytop was built to accommodate those who wished to vacation in sin is debatable.

While Skytop enjoyed a reputation for frivolity at the outset, ironically, many decades later, it suffered a comparatively conservative reputation. Public perception can be tricky, and responding to it successfully can be a dicey proposition. It was 1987, for example, when Skytop decided to bring televisions into the guest rooms. Whichever way the winds of opinion have blown over the years, Skytop continues to draw people, primarily families.

Skytop is not technically a family-run business; it is a corporation and always has been. However, four key families have been involved with Skytop from the beginning and remain so today. The Myers, Price, Smith, and White families have influenced Skytop as active board members, employees, and guests and have devoted much of their lives to promoting and preserving Skytop. It is 90 years since incorporation, and the third generation of Skytoppers now brings their grandchildren to the Pine Room for dancing on Saturday nights.

This book takes a look at some of the people credited with starting the Skytop project and necessarily focuses on activities and events during the 1930s as the balance of the photographic record is from those years.

The ingredients that came together in 1925 to form Skytop were one part people, one part place, and one part the times. Each facet is well represented in these pages.

One

"HIGH IN THE POCONOS"

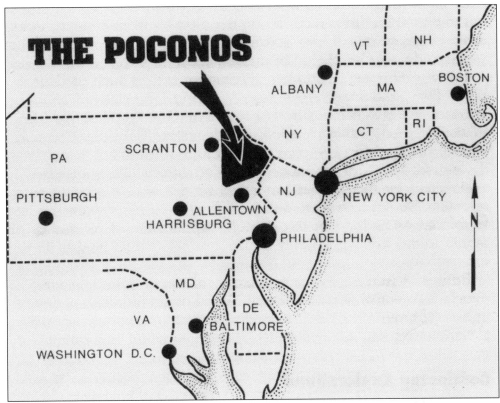

The Poconos, often referred to as mountains, are really a raised plateau, carved down over eons by glaciers and water. Although the average highest elevation measures only 2,200 feet, Skytop Lodge's first advertisements lured people to a higher altitude with their oft-repeated slogan, "Skytop Lodge—High in the Poconos." Since the Industrial Revolution, this 2,000-square-mile area has proven a bastion of fresh air and recreation to urban dwellers of the Northeast. (Courtesy of Rutgers University Press.)

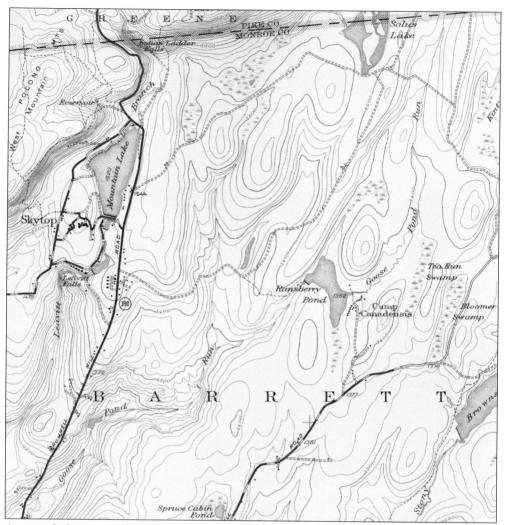

A magnified section of a 1943 USGS quadrangle shows Skytop property in the upper left-hand corner. It is helpful to orient new and old Skytoppers alike to some of the land features of Skytop as well as some of the names of those features. The large lake visible on the right when driving into Skytop is officially Mountain Lake but appears as Skytop Lake in brochures. Originally marsh and swamp, this lake is manmade. Dammed by early homesteaders, it was later enlarged by Skytop in the 1930s. The edge of the Pocono escarpment is illustrated in this topographical map by the tightly grouped contour lines in the upper left-hand corner. Here, they are labeled West and East Mountain. For years, Skytop has called East Mountain, Skytop Mountain. Also clearly illustrated is Salus Lake. Before and after this map, this body of water has been called Goose Pond. Skytop property straddles both Monroe and Pike Counties, but the majority lies in Barrett Township, Monroe County.

Parting of the Ways, Canadensis, Pa.

The tattered photograph above from around 1915 shows the intersection at the crossroads in Canadensis. The narrow strip of road disappearing into the distance in the center is the road leading to Skytop. Two decades later, that area looked a bit more like the postcard image below. The vantage of the image below differs by 90 degrees and shows modern-day Route 447 looking north. The right-hand turn to Skytop would have been beyond the Brown's building (at right). Downtown Canadensis in this era had far more commerce than now. (Both, courtesy of the Barrett Township Historical Society.)

One of the many challenges faced by Skytop Lodge developers was the condition of the public roads, such as the one shown above. This road cut through Skytop property from east to west in 1925 and exemplifies what Claudia Malleson brings to life in the following passage: "The road they traveled that fateful summer day in 1925 was horrible. The car lurched and crashed over boulders and potholes. A cloud of dust followed them up the steep grade, three miles out of Canadensis. The driver, Sam Packer, was young, good-looking, and full of enthusiasm for the project at hand. As he drove north, Packer smiled while thinking of his dream to manage a brand-new, first-rate, resort hotel in the Poconos." (Courtesy of the National Park Service, Frederick Law Olmsted National Historic Site.)

Above is the old stone arch bridge (now concrete) at the north end of Skytop Lake. Partially visible on the left is the Mountain Lake House. (Courtesy of the National Park Service, Frederick Law Olmsted National Historic Site.)

The Mountain Lake House, pictured here in the early 1920s, is located at the northern end of Mountain Lake (Skytop Lake). In a sense, the Mountain Lake House was one of the forerunners of Skytop Lodge. Proprietor Frank Janney originally catered to trout fisherman but had begun advertising year-round accommodations and promoting tobogganing, skiing, and other winter activities. Historically, this homestead had long been a stopping place for travelers coming over the mountain. A few miles south were tanneries in Mountainhome and Canadensis, and a few miles north was a gristmill in Greentown. For 3¢, a man passing through could buy a glass of whiskey here. When Sam Packer was trying to assemble the tracts of land that make up the Skytop estate, the parcel belonging to the Janneys was the most necessary, as it contained the lake. The Janneys were one of the last landowners to sell to Packer. Subsequently, the couple opened another boardinghouse closer to Cresco called the Pleasant Ridge House. The structure shown here, often called the Jenny House, remained part of Skytop, housing employees until it was demolished in the 1950s. (Courtesy of the Barrett Township Historical Society.)

Before there was Skytop, there was Buck Hill Falls, Skytop's other predecessor. Skytop Lodge cannot deny its Quaker roots as its first general manager, Samuel H. Packer, had been the assistant manager here and his uncle Charles Thompson, the manager. This Quaker resort was founded in 1901 and catered to the Hicksite branch of Philadelphia Quakers. Many of Buck Hill's guests and patrons became patrons and investors in Skytop Lodge. Skytop's growth and success were clearly built upon the reputation that had been proven at Buck Hill Falls. While Buck Hill Falls has since closed and the structure pictured here remains empty, there was a long relationship between the two resorts, both personal and public. Rivalries and competitions were constant, and the two companies each tried to use these to their own advantage. (Courtesy of the Buck Hill Falls Archives.)

In Frederic W. Smith's book *Skytop: An Adventure*, he explains the naming of Skytop Lodge. Prior to construction of the lodge, the original investors were together at a meeting, and Smith reports: "Recalling that upon the scenic Smiley estate at Lake Mohonk, New York, the highest promontory was known as Sky Top, I proposed that we might use those two words and name our company and building 'Sky Top Lodge.'" The image above is a 1920s photograph of that promontory in New York. Early Mohonk brochures (1873) claim the word *mohonk* is in fact an Indian word meaning "on the great Sky Top." Guests frequently compare the two properties without realizing the connection. (Courtesy of the Mohonk Mountain House Archives.)

Despite the discontinuity in this manually created panoramic, it successfully captured the landscape as it was when Skytop Lodge was being built. To become oriented to this vista, note the lodge under construction at the far right. From this point, the view then pans from north to west and then south as one's eye moves to the left. The remnant snow on the ground and the

April 17th, 1928.

Mr. A. F. Borth,
Market St. Title & Trust Co.,
52nd & Market Sts.,
Phila., Pa.

Dear Mr. Borth:

Under separate cover, I am sending you photographs taken around SKYTOP during the latter part of January.

As soon as we have some up-to-date photographs taken, I will see that you are supplied. Might I suggest that you show these to Mr. Diesel?

The three panoramas when placed together, given an excellent idea of the country surrounding SKYTOP from the Lodge looking south toward Delaware Water Gap.

This series of photographs were taken directly in back of my house.

Yours very truly,

SKYTOP LODGES, INC.,

SHP:PAW.

Sam. H. Packer, Gen. Mgr.

This 1928 letter confirms that the panoramas were taken by Samuel Packer.

stage of construction suggest this was taken in the late winter or early spring of 1928. Captions written on the back specify that there is a small lake between the camera and the snowbank and a golf course on the other side of the snowbank. The notation on the left-hand side of the image indicates the 14th fairway is in the foreground and the ninth fairway and green beyond.

The picture above was taken in March 1927 from the construction site and looks north toward West Mountain (left) and Skytop Mountain (right). Skytop Lake is at center. (Courtesy of Lucille May and Kendric Packer.)

Construction on the golf course began a year earlier than the lodge in a successful effort to have it open when the first guests arrived. This is a rare photograph taken of the property in 1926, before the lodge was constructed. The patchwork of farms and homesteads purchased to form the Skytop holdings are evident against the rough early grading of the Robert White–designed 18-hole golf course. White was a native of St. Andrews, Scotland, and came to the United States to study agronomy. Like many early golf professionals, he made his own clubs, taught golf, designed some golf courses, and consulted on others. His true passion and training was in grass and turf management. He was also the first president and founder of the PGA. (Courtesy of Lucille May and Kendric Packer.)

Started in April 1927 and finished by June 1928, it took just 14 months to complete the lodge. The dining room was enlarged after the first season with additional rooms above. Considering it was 1925 when Skytop first incorporated, it took longer to purchase all the property, solicit investors, and hire the golf course architect, building architect, landscape designers, and construction company than it took to construct the structure. The influx of building materials shipped via railroad was so great, an additional siding was constructed and partially financed by Skytop to better accommodate the amount of arriving freight.

Both of these photographs were taken during the later stages of lodge construction in February 1928. In the picture above, the photographer is facing south looking at the front, or north face, of the lodge. The porte cochere has not yet been built, and only the framework of the widow's walk is in place. On the left-hand side of the image, sharp eyes can make out workers on the fifth level as well as on the roof. In the image below, the photographer is looking northeast at the south side of the lodge. At this point in time, the south porch is not in the construction plans, having been removed in an effort to reduce costs. (Both, courtesy of Lucille May and Kendric Packer.)

The sketch above, drawn by architect John Muller, is from an early pamphlet developed to attract investors. Sky Top Lodges, Inc., was the name used to incorporate the operating company in July 1925. At the same time, a holding company, the Pocono Hotels Corporation, also incorporated. Stock was sold in the Pocono Hotel Corporation. Once actively in business, the operating company name quickly became one word, as shown on the luggage tag below.

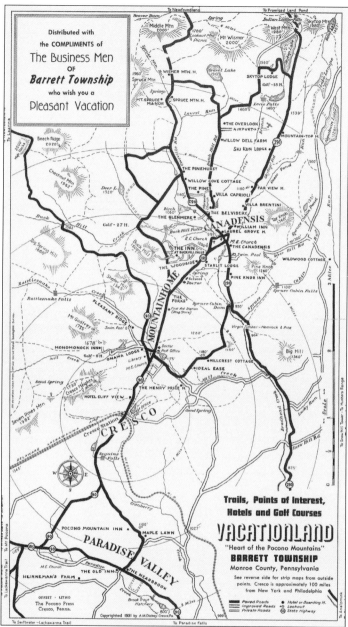

This 1931 "Business Men of Barrett Township" brochure maps the incredible number of hotels, inns, and boardinghouses that existed in an area less than 10 square miles. Due in equal parts to the railroad and the prosperity that followed World War I, Barrett Township (which includes Buckhill, Canadensis, Cresco, Mountainhome, and Skytop) had evolved into a service economy. Farming families were now subsidizing their income working in this fledgling resort industry. Within six miles of Skytop, a traveler could stay at no less than 20 different establishments. Except for Skytop, all of these resort have undergone closure and/or changes in ownership. A few of the structures still stand, such as the Pinehurst, but are private homes or apartments. Sadly, many such as the Onowa Lodge and Monomonock Inn were dramatically lost to fire. Only Skytop Lodge has endured, the sole vestige of Vacationland.

22

Two

FOUNDERS
AND FINANCIERS

Opening day, June 16, 1928, is captured in this image. Shaking hands on the left is Daniel White, financial investor and Skytop Club president. On the right is Charles N. Thompson, first chairman of Skytop Lodge's board of directors and general manager of the nearby Buck Hill Falls Inn. Behind Thompson and to the far right is Skytop Lodge general manager Sam Packer, nephew of Charles Thompson. (Courtesy of Lucille May and Kendric Packer.)

Skytop Lodge's first general manager, Samuel H. "Sam" Packer, was born in 1889 and died in 1944. He was a great-nephew to Asa Packer, who founded Lehigh Valley University and ran the Lehigh Valley Railroad. Sam Packer worked at Buck Hill Falls Inn Company for 16 years before the Skytop Lodge project began. He was the man on the ground, coordinating people and assembling the land needed to make this dream resort come true. His promotions of and dedication to Skytop were tireless. No opportunity was overlooked in searching for both investors and potential customers, and he was equally ceaseless in his efforts to entertain the guests he did attract. Though he left Skytop to run the Lake Placid Club in 1935, his influence on the early development of Skytop was fundamental to its success. In the image below, Packer sits in a glider he both built and flew in 1925. (Below, courtesy of Lucille May and Kendric Packer.)

The image at right shows Sam Packer standing in front of the northwest corner of the lodge with his two children, Margaret Packer and Samuel H. Packer II (facing the camera), during the cornerstone ceremony marking Skytop Lodge's grand opening. According to local newspaper accounts, thousands were in attendance to witness the event and tour the new million-dollar resort. Visible in images and footage taken during the event, coins and other items were placed inside the cornerstone marked 1927, the year construction commenced. In 1957, when construction began on the Laurel Room addition, a new precast cornerstone was ordered. The roof of the Laurel Room meets at precisely the spot of the original cornerstone, the northwest corner of the lodge. It is not known if the addition covered up the original stone, or if it was removed during the process. (Right, courtesy of Lucille May and Kendric Packer; below, courtesy of the National Park Service, Frederick Law Olmsted National Historic Site.)

Pictured here is Lucille Taylor Packer, wife of general manager Samuel H. Packer. Before marrying, Lucille had earned a contract with the New York Metropolitan Opera House. Rather than pursue this career path, she moved to the Poconos, started a family, and limited her singing engagements to audiences at Skytop Lodge. The very first night the lodge opened, she is listed as a performer. Another lesser-known title held by Lucille Packer was postmaster. Skytop Lodge established a post office in 1928, and while the location within the building has moved, it has remained in continuous operation. Below is the whole Packer family in the early 1930s. The children are, from front to back, Lucille Packer, Kendric Packer, and Samuel H. Packer II. Sadly, Lucille and Sam's first-born child, Margaret, died at age four from pneumonia. (Both, courtesy of Lucille May and Kendric Packer.)

Barclay White was active on Skytop's board of directors for 47 years. He was a Philadelphia Quaker and nephew of another Skytop investor, Daniel S. White. An avid fishermen and golfer, the younger White can be credited with bringing golf pro Harold Callaway to Skytop. (Courtesy of the Barclay White family.)

Instrumental in the development of Skytop Lodge, Barclay White first became involved when his construction company won the bid to build Skytop Lodge. He was also partnered in the development of the Barrett Airport and several cottages on the property, one of which is still owned by his descendants.

Raymond Price was an important figure in the creation of Skytop Lodge. As a descendant of John Price, the pioneer who first settled the area around Skytop in 1761, the Price family owned much of the land in the community. In 1913, Raymond Price opened a Ford Motor Company dealership in Mountainhome, a location about halfway between Skytop property and Cresco's train station. He provided car service to arriving passengers and grew his business around the thriving Pocono resorts. Sam Packer, fellow World War I veteran and Mountainhome basketball teammate, was a peer of Price. These two men shared a passion for cars and were involved daily in shepherding Skytop Lodge from idea to physical reality. In exchange for stock in the Pocono Hotel Corporation, Price provided equipment needed for construction of the lodge and development of the land. (Courtesy of Phyllis Spooner Price.)

It is to Fredric W. Smith that this author and the public owe a debt of gratitude, as it was his 1963 account, *SKYTOP: An Adventure*, that created the record of Skytop. A successful attorney and president of the National Council of the YMCA, Smith became a single father of two young children when his wife died of encephalitis in 1922. Grief-stricken by the loss of his wife, Smith followed the advice of Dr. Earl Mayne, a close personal friend and physician, and invested his energies and focus on a project. When the two men were introduced to the idea of building a hotel on the scrub brush–covered Pocono plateau, they were less than impressed; however, after several more visits and discussions, Smith and Mayne agreed to partner in the project. Smith acted as chief counsel and financial overseer, spending many late nights reconciling inventories and cost accounts. He served as secretary treasurer of the original board of directors, chairman of the board, and president of Skytop Club during the first 40 years of the Skytop story.

Shown here in his later years on top of Skytop Mountain, Dr. Earl Mayne was closely involved with the Skytop project from its earliest inception. A financial investor, active board member, and generally influential man, he grew up in the Midwest, becoming an engineer and practicing in that field to finance his medical education. After becoming a doctor, he and his author-painter wife, Maud Rittenhouse, moved to Brooklyn, New York, where he successfully practiced medicine for more than 50 years. Mayne served on the board of the Pocono Hotels Corporation as well as on the board of the Skytop Club. He was responsible for guiding the construction of Skytop's hiking trails as well as establishing Skytop's Maintain Your Health Department and solaria. From its opening until the late 1980s, Skytop had a full-time doctor or nurse on staff to tend to any of the guests' medical needs. (Courtesy of Miriam Mayne Griswold.)

This gentleman was a key financial investor in Skytop Lodge. Daniel S. White, together with J.C. Myers, put up $200,000 in collateral to secure Skytop's second mortgage. This was essential security needed before construction on the hotel could begin in April 1927. Daniel White was president of the largest hotel in Atlantic City, the Traymore. As an experienced hotelier, he prescribed reinforced concrete construction at Skytop to reduce both the possibility of fire and also the public fear of it, enabling the hotel to advertise this advantage. Reinforced concrete was a relatively new material that White had successfully used 10 years earlier, enlarging the Traymore to rival his cousin's hotel, the Marlborough Blenheim. A surviving registration card documents the White's stay the first night the lodge opened. (Right, courtesy of the Barclay White family.)

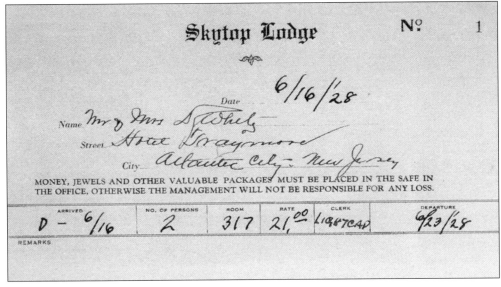

Skytop Lodge   № 1

Date 6/16/28

Name Mr & Mrs D. White
Street Hotel Traymore
City Atlantic City — New Jersey

MONEY, JEWELS AND OTHER VALUABLE PACKAGES MUST BE PLACED IN THE SAFE IN THE OFFICE, OTHERWISE THE MANAGEMENT WILL NOT BE RESPONSIBLE FOR ANY LOSS.

ARRIVED	NO. OF PERSONS	ROOM	RATE	CLERK	DEPARTURE
D - 6/16	2	317	21,00	LIGHTCAP	6/23/28

REMARKS

Jacob Christian "Jake" Myers was one of two Atlantic City hoteliers to contribute his experience, capital, and future to Skytop Lodge. Myers bought property in Atlantic City with his brother and brother in-law and built the Hotel Chelsea in 1900. Pictured here as a young man, Myers was responsible for the immediate decision to enlarge Skytop's dining room space after its very first season. He was generally very involved in the kitchen and is credited for the early success of Skytop's cuisine. Additionally, his Atlantic City connections helped secure provisions during the lean rationing years of World War II. (Both, courtesy of Eve Myers Doherty.)

Three

ARRIVALS
AND DEPARTURES

The family in this 1930s photograph remains unidentified. Lynn Derby Graham describes arriving at Skytop: "We arrived family en masse with two cars and two chauffeurs; some coming in by train to be met in Cresco. The most exciting part was coming through the gate and the first glimpse of the Lodge—'high on the hill'—Being greeted on the north porch . . . the hordes of luggage quickly sorted by room and person; trunks for each person were sent ahead and claimed-all to be waiting in our rooms after lunch. Our arrival was always timed for noon-lunch and then an afternoon of unpacking and arranging."

7-24-1916   From Steamtown NHS Archives C3602

Alongside every successful business is a transportation system that connects the consumers to the product. In the case of Skytop Lodge, and for that matter all the rooming houses and hotels that blossomed in Cresco during the early part of the century, it was the railroad that ferried in the clientele. Cresco Station served the town of Oakland, which was later renamed Cresco, with service from the Delaware, Lackawanna & Western (DL&W). Cresco's station is six miles south of Skytop Lodge. The freight-handling business peaked between 1926 and 1932, as Buck Hill, Skytop, and other smaller hotels were being developed and started taking in guests. However, the second peak occurred from 1936 to 1945, during the Great Depression and into the period of World War II. (Both, courtesy of the Steamtown National Archives.)

7-24-16   From Steamtown NHS Archives   C. 3599

A 1998 quarterly newsletter of the Barrett Township Historical Society stated about the history of the Cresco Station: "The 'Lackawanna Limited' with the famous 'Phoebe Snow' would pull into Cresco Station on a Friday evening disgorge 1,800 people and retrieve them again on Sunday to return to the cities for the next week's work." Travel to Skytop from New York was direct along the DL&W, while the trip from Philadelphia required a transfer in Manuka Chunk, New Jersey. Gas rationing during World War II increased passenger service, and businesses near train stations flourished. Often mothers and children stayed in the country and only the fathers returned to the city, particularly in the summers. (Courtesy of the Barrett Township Historical Society.)

All manner of vehicles were employed to go to the station to pick up and drop off guests travelling back to the cities. Each of the larger resorts would have a spot at the station and a sign for passengers to indicate where to wait for the arriving shuttle. During winter weather conditions, sleds had occasion to provide this service. During the rationing of World War II, it is recalled that vehicles would coast down Krummell Hill Road as far as possible to conserve precious gasoline.

Travel to the Poconos was the thing to do not only during the summer season, but also during the wintertime. These so-called snow trains would serve the area as winter sports became a favorite pastime for the people of the large northeastern population. (Courtesy of Thomas Skeans.)

In the late 1930s, Skytop occasionally made arrangements to host snow weekends for private schools and colleges, arranging for special train trips around Presidents' Day. The horse-drawn sleds would bring guests to the slopes or down to other scheduled events held on the lower lake.

Motoring To The Skytop Club "High In The Poconos"

Mileage

Philadelphia To Skytop	105	Miles
Harrisburg " "	123	"
Lancaster " "	137	"
Williamsport " "	118	"
Altoona " "	220	"
Pittsburg " "	285	"
Franklin " "	265	"
Erie " "	320	"
New York City " "	105	"

After World War I, automobile ownership skyrocketed. While railroads provided major arteries through rural areas, once a station or depot was established, the automobile provided a comfortable ride to distances beyond. Automobile clubs, rather than railroad companies, began to furnish hotel guides. Skytop's location, roughly 100 miles from two major cities, had and continues to have major appeal. According to authors of *The Poconos: An Illustrated Natural History*, "About fifty percent of the population of the United States lives within a six hour drive of the Poconos."

In the 1934 scene above, the Kerr family of New Jersey is shown departing under Skytop's porte cochere. Closest to the Pierce Arrow on the left is 10-year-old Herbert Kerr. Next to him is seven-year-old Samuel Kerr. Standing behind the boys is their mother, Elizabeth Sinclair Kerr, and their grandmother Bessie Sinclair. New Jersey governor Robert Meyner, who served from 1954 to 1962, stands behind this group next to the pillar.

Barclay White of the Barclay White construction company, who was himself a pilot, joined capital and equipment with Raymond Price to construct the Barrett Airport, located adjacent and just south of Skytop property. Following the same formula of selling stock and soliciting investors, the airport was laid out in 1931 and served as way for guests to arrive as well as a site for popular stunt shows, fly-ins, and scenic tours. The image above is likely of sightseers around 1933. A well-respected glider pilot and soaring expert named Lew Barringer organized the first air shows at Skytop. He wrote about a weekend fly-in to Skytop that he called Pocono Picnic, during which a glider, piloted by Jack O'Meara, broke the world glider record by performing 43 consecutive back loops before landing on the fairway directly in front of the lodge. The 53-acre Barrett Airport still functions as a public airport, though it is no longer owned by Skytop.

This image captures the serene beauty of Skytop Lake. Lindbergh's transatlantic flight in 1927 triggered widespread interest in aviation. Pilots would put down a ship in just about any field (or lake) they could. Newspapers captured Vic Sommers landing his WACO biplane on Skytop's front lawn a month after it opened in 1928. In 1933, it cost $28 for two people to catch a ride from New York to the Barrett Airport in a plane with a cabin, $15 in a plane with an open cockpit.

In this 1933 photograph, Peck Rake is driving, Louise Raney is in the dogsled, and her 10-year-old son Quin Raney is standing alongside. The plane and this company are all on the frozen Skytop Lake with East Mountain in the background.

A 1930s brochure promoting bountiful game at Skytop depicts an autogiro in the south lawn. Positively identified in this photograph is Pop Roberts, second from the left, and Woody Gravel, third from left. The autogiro was a popular predecessor to the modern helicopter, and the pilot pictured here, second from right, may be a man named Charles Otto. Skytop employees were hired to drive (or flush) the deer toward guests who had come to hunt and catch large game.

Four

THE LODGE

John Stubbs, a New York securities dealer and guest at Buck Hill Falls, was the one man connecting all the other investors. It was Stubbs who recommended New York architect John Muller to design the lodge. Muller's use of gambrel rooflines may have been influenced by their appearance locally, though nothing, of course, existed on this scale. The choice of native fieldstone effectively connects the building to the landscape and creates the impression that the structure belongs on that spot. (Courtesy of Eve Myers Doherty.)

SKY-TOP LODGES CANADENSIS-PA. ROSSITER·AND·MULLER (ASSOCIATED) 15 WEST 5
MORTIMER·FOSTER (ARCHITECTS) NEW·YOR

These drawings were done in June 1926. One of the features that makes Skytop Lodge stand out when contrasted with Buck Hill Falls and Pocono Manor is the building itself. Skytop was planned on a grand scale, commensurate with the life and times of the mid-1920s. Buck Hill Falls and Pocono Manor were built in 1901 and 1902, respectively, and began as small, 20-room structures that expanded over the years. Likewise, Mohonk Mountain House grew as a series of structures added

SKY-TOP LODGES ~ CANADENSIS·PA. ROSSITER·AND·MULLER (ASSOCIATE
MORTIMER·FOSTER (ARCHITECT

SCALE.
1 INCH = 8 FEET.

NORTH ELEVATION.

on over time. While Skytop's main lodge has had four primary additions, the last of which occurred in 2004, the overall line and shape of the building has remained consistent. Guests who have met Skytop as children return years later with their own children, and this long-standing structure greets them in way that is familiar and inviting. The Rossiter and Muller design achieved the quality of immortality to those who know it well. (Both, courtesy of Eric Woodward Architect.)

ST 38 TH STREET.
YORK CITY. N.Y.

SCALE.
1 INCH = 8 FEET.

SOUTH · ELEVATION.

These long views of the north porch captured from opposing ends illustrate the vast piazza as it was originally intended. Note how the porch extends fully open to both the east and the west. Practicality overruled aesthetic twice in this porch's history. The first challenge came from the north wind. Habitual Pocono winter weather blew snowdrifts onto the porch with such regularity that an unattractive temporary enclosure was erected for protection. The second broach came in the 1940s when storage and utility needs brought stone enclosures to each end of the porch. (Above, courtesy of the Barclay White family.)

These pictures of the south porch were taken before the windows and doors were installed. The south porch was planned, removed from the plans, then deemed necessary to the overall scheme in April 1928, three months before the grand opening. This explains why there are not yet windows and doors in the courtyard. Note the railing above the porch and the golf house that are no longer extant. (Both, courtesy of the Barclay White family.)

SKYTOPICS

VOLUME XV · No. 1   WINTER 1943 · 1944

PLAN A *Sunshine* VACATION

The next best thing to that Southern trip or cruise which you can't take this winter, will be a Skytop "Sunshine" vacation. The Vita-glass windbreaks of the enlarged enclosure on our South veranda admit 78% of the healthful actinic rays of the sun, while you are sitting

(OVER)

In the early years of Skytop, a newsletter called *Skytopics* was circulated. Only a few examples remain available from the early 1930s and two from the period of World War II. Production seemed to have ended with the war. In the example above, the image depicts people sunbathing on the south porch with the help of Vita Glass. Vita Glass was installed there as well as on the fifth floor in the solaria. As part of the Maintain Your Health program, guests were invited to reap the benefits of this healthful remedy.

The Pine Room, or main lobby of the lodge, measures 112 feet across and has not been altered significantly in 86 years. While some of the upholstered furniture, draperies, and rugs have changed, many of the chairs, tables, and end tables are original. The photograph above was taken in 1928, and the image below showcases Christmas decorations in 1933. The pine paneling and large fireplace can be credited to Sam Packer. They were signature elements he preferred using to create an inviting and comfortable space. (Above, courtesy of the Barclay White family; below, courtesy of Lucille May and Kendric Packer.)

Skytop is pictured here around 1930. After the first season of business, Jake Myers knew that the dining room space needed to be enlarged if the hotel was going to be successful. Shown here is that extension, as it was appointed for the Christmas season. Locally harvested evergreens decorated the arched transom, and the center runner extended through both wooden-floored rooms. (Courtesy of Lucille May and Kendric Packer.)

Pictured here is the charter meeting of Barrett Lions Club on Halloween night in 1949. Though this image was captured as two separate photographs that do not match seamlessly, it still illustrates the Myers extension and the original decor. Hardwood floors have since been covered, and air-conditioning units changed the ceiling; however, key elements such as the arched windows and columns remain the same, making the room instantly recognizable. (Courtesy of the Barrett Township Historical Society.)

This photograph from an early advertisement shows clean and simply appointed guest rooms. The decor for the lodge was touted as Early American and befitting a relaxed atmosphere. In the 1950s, a lengthy renovation of guest rooms created private baths for the 20 percent of rooms that previously shared bathrooms. According to the rate sheet below, in 1929 two people could stay in a room such as this for $15. Meals on the American plan were $1.25 for breakfast, $2 for lunch, and $2.50 for dinner. Originally staff and servants of guests were housed on the fourth floor. After the first season, staff dormitories were added to the property.

SKYTOP LODGE

1929   DAILY RATES   *1929*   AMERICAN PLAN

A discount of 10% from daily rates on stay of one week or longer.

Classification of Rooms as per Floor Plans	November - December March - April (Holidays Excepted)		January - February May - June - October (Including Holidays)		July - August September	
	One Person	Two Persons	One Person	Two Persons	One Person	Two Persons
H	6.00		7.00		8.00	
G	7.00		9.00		10.00	
F	8.00		10.00		12.00	
E		12.00		13.00		15.00
D		13.00		15.00		16.00
C		16.00		18.00		19.00
B		18.00		20.00		22.00
A		20.00		23.00		25.00
AA		20.00		23.00		28.00

The charge for a fractional part of a day, after the first day's stay, will be one-quarter, one-half and three-quarters of the rate quoted. Full charge for period of reservation will be made unless cancellation is received seven days in advance of starting date. Second person in single room, add $7.00. Third person in double room, add one-half double rate up to $8.00. Children under 6 years, $4.00 per day. Maids and Chauffeurs, in Dormitory, $6.00 per day. OVER

The Tea Room underneath the south porch still has that 1930s feel to it. The large window on the right has been filled in and is now covered by a large shelving unit. This space was always intended to provide guests sundry items and provide an alternate place to eat when the Windsor Dining Room was closed. Often, seating would be provided in the courtyard. The adjoining space under the center portion of the south porch has long been a rental room for activities equipment, but at present, it is the Skytop flower shop. (Courtesy of Lucille May and Kendric Packer.)

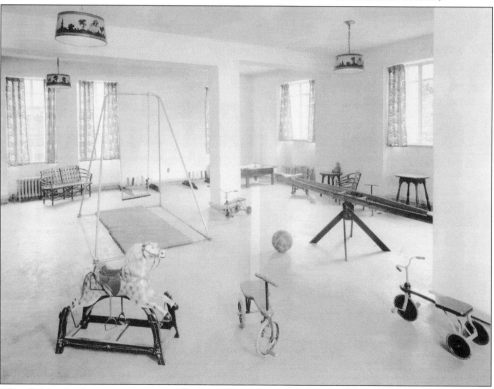

The children's playroom was originally located off the entertainment room in the space currently occupied by billiard tables. A portion of the original space shown here has also been converted to offices. The windows seen in this photograph have been obscured from public access. Brochures illustrating this children's play area reflect the sentiment of the times, stating simply, "Here the younger guests may play, undisturbed and undisturbing." (Courtesy of the Barclay White family.)

The room now home to miniature golf, table tennis, and video games was initially billed as an entertainment room. Many of Skytop's theatrical revues were held here. Above is a long shot, taken in 1928, looking east toward the fireplace. Seen in this image is the more spacious original interior that existed before the current gift shop and dance floor were installed. First-run movies were shown in this space every week. Chairs were arranged for the viewing as seen in the photograph below, taken from the opposite end of the room about 1956. (Above, courtesy of the Barclay White family.)

These two 1948 photographs depict the gift shop that existed from the mid-1940s to the early 1990s. The space shown here is the present Laurel Lounge. Evelyn Myers, daughter-in-law of early founder and investor Jake Myers, owned this shop for 20 years, and Eleanor Biles ran the shop afterward for another 20 years. Customarily, ladies would come over from Buck Hill Falls for the day. They would have lunch, get their hair done, and shop here for wedding and anniversary gifts such as fine sets of silver or crystal. (Both, courtesy of Eve Myers Doherty.)

The gift shop shown in the photograph above predates the 1948 images on the previous page. Here, the space is deeper and extends into what is now part of the Tap Room. The door into the Tap Room may have been an entrance to this gift shop at one time.

This is the only image of an early linen shop that existed underneath the south porch, adjacent to the Tea Room. A different photograph taken of the courtyard area outside this store reveals a sign that reads, "Art Linen Shoppe Sports Dresses." The majority of this space now constitutes Skytop's flower shop.

This room, with an identical footprint to the library above it, is the club room. Pictured here are two vastly different incarnations of the club room. Above is an image from 1928, when the lodge opened, while the image below was captured 30 years later. Curiously, floor plans from 1926 label this large space "Ladies Room." Skytop Club members have made use of this room for a variety of purposes over the years, most notoriously as a bar. Supplying liquor in this room, only to Skytop Club members, provided a way around Pennsylvania's state laws banning Sunday liquor sales. (Above, courtesy of the Barclay White family.)

Seen above is the two-lane bowling alley that was constructed the year the lodge opened. According to an early plat of the property and proposed cottage lots, the bowling alley was located near the early tennis courts, approximately the site of the contemporary Streamside Cottage. An anecdote from a gentleman who stayed at Skytop during Prohibition claimed that if a guest desired a drink at that time, he could call down to the front desk and say that he wanted to go bowling. In short order, a bowling bag of hooch would be brought up to the room. Below is the portion of the entertainment room that is currently occupied by the gift shop. (Both, courtesy of the Barclay White family.)

This picture of the Skytop staff was taken about 1940. All personnel were strictly managed and held to a high standard of service, which was regulated to the smallest detail. During the depths of the Depression and also World War II, staff was cut to a bare minimum, particularly during the winter. Portions of the building were closed to minimize heating costs, and front of house duties, such as front desk and telephone operator, were performed by only one person.

Five

THE LANDSCAPE

Skytop Lodge property was selected specifically for its diverse physical attributes. When working at Buck Hill Falls, Sam Packer frequently led guests on hikes to the vistas and waterfalls of Skytop. Shown here is Indian Ladder Falls around 1928. The most-frequented waterfall, due to its easier access, this three-tiered cataract pleases even the most disinterested straggler. (Courtesy of the Barclay White family.)

The entire vista south of the lodge is free of any tall trees in this 1928 image. Anyone sitting on the south porch could see all the way across the valley south and west to the Delaware Water Gap. Note the cottages in the upper left-hand corner, which were built concurrently with the lodge. A small house in the center of the photograph roughly marks the location founders anticipated the lodge would be constructed. Behind this house to the south is a spectacular ravine and Leavitt Falls, then known as Devil's Hole. When standing on the edge of this ravine, the effect of this drop-off was thought to be quite an advantage. Landscape architects from Olmsted Brothers surprised everyone when they decided against building on the edge of the ravine. They pointed out the multiple advantages of the "northern site such as; a view of Mountain Lake, a backdrop of mountain ridges, and the cultivation of the south lawn as a backyard." (Courtesy of the Barclay White family.)

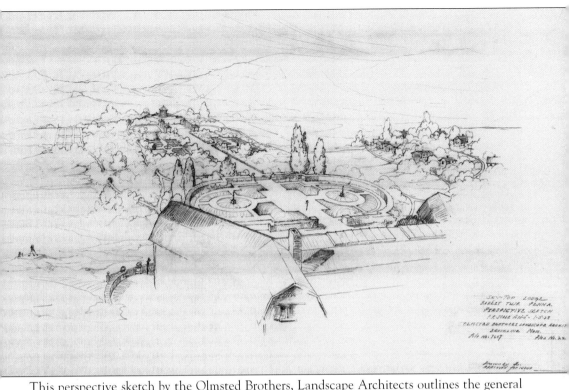

This perspective sketch by the Olmsted Brothers, Landscape Architects outlines the general plan intended for the south garden. Between the time Packer signed the first deeds and the time construction began, the property had become untenably overgrown. Development of the area immediately surrounding the hotel was critical. Carefully graded walkways extending out from the south porch were stymied by changes to the construction plan and the late decision to add that porch. A companion list of native plantings that were sourced locally included mountain laurel, rhododendrons, evergreens, hemlock, dogwoods, viburnums, juniper, and azaleas. Their design called for plantings that ranged in height from hardy ground covers and rock plants to varieties projected to provide shade, eventually. Pressure was great. Construction was ongoing up until the scheduled opening, and the men from Olmsted Brothers were contending with trucks, scaffolding, mud, and Mother Nature. Continued tree planting and landscaping extended well into subsequent seasons. (Courtesy of the National Park Service, Frederick Law Olmsted National Historic Site.)

This dam across the lower swimming lake, shown here around 1928, was initially constructed by the Levis Falls Rod and Gun Club, of which Sam Packer was the secretary. This club amassed the first 500 acres that were to be the seed property around which the Skytop holdings would spread. Once Packer had secured promises from adjacent landholders that they would sell to him, the rod and gun club said they would allow their 500 acres to be included in the project. The length and breadth of these negotiations and manipulations took several years. At one juncture, Packer left town and moved to New Jersey in an attempt to quell rumors of development and force down the inflated asking prices. (Above, courtesy of Kendric Packer and Lucille May.)

At right is Leavitt Falls, and below is the lower pool that forms farther downstream. Before this section was purchased by Skytop, it belonged to the Levis Falls Rod and Gun Club. Before the club owned it, Eleazer Price had a sawmill along this branch of the stream. The mill is now gone; however, an old icehouse still stands near the trailhead leading to the falls. In the lodge's early years, ice was harvested from the lower lake and stored in sawdust. Rural electrification and refrigeration were recent advents in northeastern Pennsylvania. The Wallenpaupack hydroelectric dam had just been completed in 1926. (Both, courtesy of the Barclay White family.)

The bridge shown here below Leavitt Falls was lost during a flood in 1955. The trail to Leavitt Falls used to traverse the stream in several places and climbed back up the glen to Leavitt Falls Road (the road parallel to the ninth fairway). After the destruction of the bridges, Skytop elected not to replace them and ceased maintenance of the trail on the north side of the branch.

The image above also dates to before 1955. Remnants of the destroyed stonework are overgrown and half submerged but still there. At one time, this picnic spot was called Indian Moccasin Spring and is across the Leavitt Branch from the icehouse. (Courtesy of the Barclay White family.)

Pictured here are Evelyn Myers and a guest fly-fishing at the base of Indian Ladder Falls around 1939. Leavitt Falls Branch (old maps label it Levis Falls) is one of five streams that cascade down the Pocono escarpment, feeding Brodhead Creek, which drains into the Delaware River. The five streams created a true fisherman's paradise. Native brook trout in a variety of colors and sizes were abundant. Intense lumbering and tanneries diminished their populations severely, as this activity destroyed the streams' protective watershed. Eventually, populations returned through state stocking programs and the maturation of a second-growth forest. Skytop stocks the Leavitt Branch annually, and many a catch has made its way to the Windsor Dining Room. (Courtesy of Eve Myers Doherty.)

Above and below are aerial photographs of Skytop taken in 1934. The original location of the tennis courts seen above is currently a parking lot. There are just three cottages along the road that now stretches between 10 cottages. Newly planted trees dot the landscape, and the lawn-bowling court has not yet been constructed. The image below shows a better view of Skytop Lake. Dusters, a lightweight sailboat built for inland waters, were very popular in the 1950s, and races were held every summer on this upper lake. The field in the lower left-hand corner is the cutting garden. (Both, courtesy of Lucille May and Kendric Packer.)

This undated rendering of the Skytop estate was done by itinerant artist Edwin D. Mott. It was used for decades as the basis upon which trail maps and guides were created to orient guests to Skytop property. His liberally construed scale and vantage offer the unusual ability to discern the topography of West Mountain (left of the lake) and Skytop Mountain (above and to the right of the lake), as well as the details of roads, trails, waterfalls, and cottages. Mott sketched in cars on the roads, horseback riders on bridle paths, and defied true scale by squeezing the airport onto the map despite its actual location, a bit farther south. The body of water to the upper right, with the small islands, shows Goose Pond before it was drained down in the 1950s.

Shown here are two of the early cottages that were constructed within the first few years of Skytop's operation. The original purpose was to generate income through property sales. A model of a cottage colony was already in place at Buck Hill Falls, the resort with which both Sam Packer and Charles Thompson were so intimately involved. Skytop founders intended to have regular guests that would spend entire summers. These cottagers could use all the amenities of the lodge, from the golf course and dining room to the hairdresser and solarium. Cottagers could also procure groceries from the lodge kitchen. (Below, courtesy of Eve Myers Doherty.)

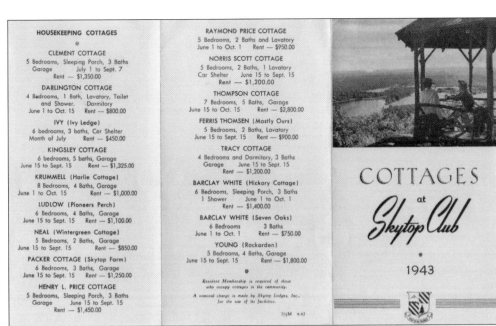

During the war, some of the homeowners let out their homes to other club members who did not own cottages at Skytop. In 1943, $1,100 could get visitors three summer months with this lovely view if one elected to stay at Pioneers Perch. This particular offering included six bedrooms, four bathrooms, and a garage. In this early view of the lodge, there are no tall pines and no ice-skating pavilion. The roadside between the window and the lodge is Dutch Hill Road, so named because of the services held in German at the Moravian church at the end of the road. At the time of this photograph, an old Bender farmhouse and barn are still standing, sectioned off from the fourth fairway.

In 1946, Skytop Lodge nearly doubled its property when the board decided to purchase land then referred to as the Personeni property. This 2,200-acre section is located on the east side of Route 390 and includes Goose Pond, formerly Salus Lake. This Goose Pond part of the property encompasses Campbell's View, the shooting range, miles of bridle paths, and the foundations of buildings that previously comprised the Personeni estate. Some of those structures are illustrated in these photographs, which accordingly date to the 1940s. This undeveloped acreage is flanked by private hunting clubs and has been historically used for hunting by Skytop guests and employees.

Initially, Skytop used the Goose Pond property primarily for recreation. The Personeni family had maintained a pristine estate that included fruit trees, a sunken garden, a canal, tennis courts, a boathouse, main house, caretaker's house, barn, and other smaller buildings. Over the years, the property hosted campouts for children, barn dances, employee housing, and boating and fishing. By the late 1960s and 1970s, the burden of road and building maintenance began to supersede usage benefits, and the structures were razed. Some residual elements remain. To the interested observer, signs of this carefully planned homestead are discernible amidst the overgrown landscape.

Skytop's original tennis courts, at Sam Packer's behest and against the Olmsted firm's advice, were located near the bowling alley, alongside the lower road that runs between the entrance dam and the lower lake. Olmsted felt the site had poor drainage, but Packer felt the trees would provide protection from winds as well as afternoon shade. During the 1955 flood caused by Hurricane Diane, this lower elevation location indeed proved devastating, as shown in the photograph below. Above is a far shot of famed tennis pro William "Big Bill" Tilden, who played at Skytop in July 1931, just days after winning the US Championship at Forest Hills. Tilden still ranks as one of the greatest tennis players of all time.

The damage caused by Hurricane Diane in 1955 was calculated by totaling the expense of the repairs, but for many, the sum of the consequences went well beyond the dollar. At the time of the storm, employees and guests could not leave the property because of the flooding at the lower elevations and lost bridges. The causeway, shown in these two photographs, and the 18th hole suffered the most costly physical damage. Skytop had been on its way to a record high occupancy that summer before the August storm struck.

When Skytop's dam was breached, the community of Canadensis, three miles to the south, endured extensive flooding. After this disaster, a dry dam was constructed just south of the Barrett Airport by the Army Corps of Engineers as a measure to prevent future devastation of this caliber.

Shown here is the east side of the lodge in 1929. In 1946, a plan was commissioned for an east wing addition. It called for 40 additional rooms and an auditorium, but it was never realized. In 1961, however, a revised addition was constructed and extended the east side of the lodge to house a natatorium, or indoor pool. The flagpole pictured here was relocated to the circle in front of the north porch. (Courtesy of Lucille May and Kendric Packer.)

Six

SKYTOP TRADITIONS

As the Olmsted firm planned and predicted, the south lawn became very much the lodge's backyard. Centered in the photograph above is the fondly remembered Skytop hostess, Catherine Twing. For over 20 years, she held court at Skytop, directing newcomers and regulars and serving tea and punch from her cart.

Held outdoors on Saturday afternoons, afternoon tea is still a Skytop tradition. In the 1950s, tea was served concurrently with putting contests and a live musical performance. Pictured here, from left to right, the violinist is likely Howard Lalley, George LeClaire is seated at the piano, and Dave Levine is on cello. This trio played regularly throughout the 1950s and 1960s.

Dances held in the Pine Room have been a Skytop tradition since the day the hotel opened in 1928. A typical Saturday night always included the sounds of a big band and the Grand March, and it still does. With roots in European and Philadelphia ballrooms, the Grand March is an intentionally simple dance designed for easy participation by all. In this early-1930s photograph, Sam Packer's alma mater, Cornell University, has graced the stage for a Halloween celebration.

Picnics were held in every season. As illustrated in these images, snow and cold were not sufficient reasons to take one's meals indoors. The picnics were regular features of a weekend at Skytop, not just special occasions or holidays. Kitchen staff prepared steak dinners and hauled their equipment to the top of Skytop Mountain while golf pro Harold Callaway shot golf balls into the valley and offered guests a chance to do the same. Later, picnics were offered on the lake at Robin Hood Dell. The Campbell family, homeowners at Skytop, particularly missed the picnic events at the top of the mountain. To keep the tradition alive, they constructed a lean-to at the site to afford any visitor adventuring to this spot a shelter in which to relax while taking in one of the best views in the Poconos.

June in the Poconos is laurel blossom time. The spectacle of the state flower in bloom was a celebrated tradition picked up by the burgeoning vacation bureau to attract tourists. Several resorts and municipalities in the area commemorated the event with pageantry, balls, and dinners, adroitly exploiting this particularly stunning time of the year. Ladies from local colleges were nominated to be queen, and for 10 days in June, a court of princesses would gather at alternating resorts while the press reported on their activities. At the end of the week, the new queen would be announced and crowned. Pictured on the left is Mildred Birchard, the 1936 laurel blossom queen, poised alongside her raison d'être at Skytop. Below are unidentified contestants.

Lawn bowling at Skytop thrived during the 1940s and 1950s. A committee formed and dedicated itself to educating guests on the game by way of pamphlets and weekly classes. Annual competitions were held every August with the team from Buck Hill Falls. A lively rivalry still exists, and the winning team displays the commemorating plaque until the next match is held. The first court was constructed in 1936. In the 1980s, it was temporarily relocated to make room for an anticipated addition. The new location met with issues that failed to sustain a sporting green, and it was subsequently restored to its original site.

A well-respected child psychologist named Dorothy Waldo Phillips was in charge of all the children during their long summer stays. Cottage children and hotel guests alike were guided by "Aunt Dorothy" in musical appreciation, arts and crafts, and Sunday school activities.

The coordinated program Aunt Dorothy created was called Camp in the Clouds, and it still exists today. Sometimes splintered into Skyteens or juniors, by the late 1930s they were headquartered in a new building down by the lake. Identified in the photograph above are Sam Packer's two sons, Kendric (left) and Samuel (second from left).

After six years orchestrating the children's activities, Aunt Dorothy wanted to record these events. After inventing a fictitious Englishwoman, she asked the Camp in the Clouds children to describe to this woman what it was like to spend the summer at a mountain resort. The result was an illustrated book, published in 1937, called *Dear Mrs. Bender*. Told from the perspective of a child, but with Aunt Dorothy's tone, observations of staff, camp activities, and life at the lodge were logged. Notable guests of the period such as Chief Justice Charles Evans Hughes, Cole Porter, and Bill Tilden are recorded here as well. In the photograph above, Aunt Dorothy (second from right) and her assistant Jeanette Palmer (right) are seated at the table. The children are, from left to right, (first row) three unidentified; (second row) unidentified, Bobby Hauptfuhrer, unidentified, Bobby Ughetta, Anne Gibson, Gloria MacCarter, and Betty Donahue; (third row) Ann Heuer, Peggy White, Dick Heuer, and Barbara Donahue.

In this 1934 photograph, some members of Camp in the Clouds are having their weekly golf lesson with golf pro Harold Callaway (second row, far right). Students in the front include, from left to right, Samuel Packer, Kendric Packer, two unidentified children, Dickie Heuer, Barbara Homer, and Peggy White. The taller boys behind remain unidentified. (Courtesy of Kendric and Lucille Packer.)

The Skytop Juniors received weekly lessons in horseback riding, golfing, or tennis. The circle inside the turnaround was the original location of a putting green that was moved to the south lawn after the first year. The hole marker on the left side of the image dates this photograph to 1928 or 1929. (Courtesy of the Barclay White family.)

Lined up in the courtyard of the south porch are the children of the cottage colony and hotel guests. This image was taken in celebration of Independence Day around 1934 and was reprinted in a *Junior Skytopics* newsletter. From left to right are Virginia Graves, unidentified, Marjorie Schlessinger, Renee Crothers, Kathryn Schlessinger, Charles Heuer, Bart Bumstead, Cecile Woodring, Ann Mordaunt, Sammy Packer, Anne Heuer, Dick Heuer, unidentified, Kenny Packer, Barbara Homer, Eddie Crothers, and Bobby Ughetta. (Courtesy of Lucille May and Kendric Packer.)

A different Fourth of July Camp in the Clouds group celebrates in a less formal pose some 20 years later. Pictured here are, from left to right, (first row) Cybil "Sibby" Callaway, Jesse ?, Bobbie Gerstell Bennet, Harold Trefethen (in wagon), Lynne Derby Graham, Holly Sawyer Augenbaugh, and Mary Malleson Briggs; (second row) Lynn Weyburn Perrine, Sally MacCorckle, Bill Malleson, Richard Wolfington, and Sue Malleson. (Courtesy of Holly Augenbaugh.)

Where we recaptured our
youth — The Circus

On more than one occasion, Skytop Lodge hosted a summer circus and Monte Carlo bazaar. Pictured above, this July 1931 event was pitched along the first fairway near the clubhouse. Acts were put on by guests and professionals alike. The event pictured below was much like a town fair, full of booths offering rummage items, ring tosses, and crafts. A car was even raffled off to the person who correctly guessed the selling price. Any proceeds from activities like these were typically donated to charities.

In this photograph, a lively entourage poses in the Windsor Dining Room around 1930. Masques and costumed events were so numerous at Skytop that some brochures mention a professional costumer being available to help guests prepare. Portrayed here are harlequins, jesters, convicts, and more. The only identified participant, looking a bit like a gypsy, is Lucille Packer, seated on the second row, far left. (Courtesy of Lucille May and Kendric Packer.)

Above, eight Skytoppers are dressed in drag around 1930. Third from the left is general manager Sam Packer. Dressing in drag reached the height of popularity in Northeastern cities during Prohibition. Chapter 5 of *Dear Mrs. Bender* discusses a Skyrackets Revue show during which "the men got dressed in girl's skirts and great big pants sticking down, danced like butterflies, were very clumsy and fell down in a pile while everybody laughed and laughed." (Courtesy of Lucille May and Kendric Packer.)

The entertainment room accommodated a stage when cottagers and guests alike joined professional talent to put on revues, musicals, and skits. The Camp in the Clouds children cultivated their own repertoire and performed plays for their parents, having worked on them during their long summer stays. Escaping the cities for cooler temperatures and clean healthy air was a lengthier affair before World War II. Families frequently stayed for several weeks, and cottagers stayed at Skytop for the summer. There was ample time to learn one's lines.

This particular pageant was an outdoor affair, held in August 1934. The water carnival, once again the brainchild of the fearless Packer, was on the lower lake and included several different floats built and constructed by cottagers and various club committees, such as the children's camp group. There were music and lights, and somehow a curtain of water was rigged for at least one of the acts. The event was open to the public to raise money for Monroe County charities. This particular float reportedly sank. Fortunately, camp children all attended swim class.

Horse races are still conducted at Skytop; however, during the contemporary version, bets are placed on small wooden horses that move along a wooden board. The photograph at right, taken in the entertainment room around 1933, shows female contestants riding much larger wooden horses as they advance along the dance floor. Arthur Murray Studio instructors were staffed in the summers to teach popular dance steps, mix the crowds, and keep people dancing; two of whom can be seen behind contestant number three.

Troupes of girls connected with Skytop either as hotel guests, regular summer cottage owners, or guests thereof would come together to perform in the annual Skyrackets Revue. Newspaper accounts use names like Skyettes and detail the dance numbers executed. Though many of the girls' names are mentioned in the papers, and certain faces appear frequently, the participants in these photographs remain unidentified.

When the lodge opened, it was fairly new to have a mountain resort open year-round. Winter activities often required some measure of physical prowess and adventuresome qualities. Dogsled rides, however, were the perfect activity for those not so athletically inclined. A guest would be wrapped in warm blankets and taken on a quiet tour of the snow-covered estate. Skytop's sled master, Julian "Peck" Rake, had a team of dogs at Skytop throughout the 1930s. Above, two unidentified people are stopped at the north porch, and Rake, seen at right, is taking a guest across the south lawn.

Sleigh rides and wagon rides have always been popular traditions at Skytop. When Skytop kept its own team of horses, the rides were horse drawn, and based on the above image even cow drawn! A tractor has since replaced the teams. Other outings, called deer jacking parties, involved the Skytop bus, mounted with an enormous spotlight, carrying guests around the property to spy on and surprise the local deer population. The image below is likely from the early 1930s. Sam Packer is standing in the back of the sleigh with a suit and overcoat on, and others are being towed on skis behind the sleigh.

Seven

TOURNAMENTS AND COMPETITIONS

Above, four women pose on the steps of the south porch after a speed-skating tournament in 1931. Contests were a regular feature at Skytop Lodge. The temptation of winning a trophy drew competitors, and competitors drew crowds. Sam Packer introduced the first-ever shooting tournament, ladies golf invitational, speed-skating competition, ice hockey meet, dogsled derby, tennis tournament, horse show, polo match, and wood-chopping contest. The glass case in the west stairwell was constructed specifically for displaying trophies.

Horseback riding at Skytop encompassed not only breakfast rides and lessons for children, but also horse shows. Pictured below is a Skytop Club member at the Pocono Mountain Horseshow, which was held annually in Mount Pocono's Arena in the Clouds. Above is the children's show at Skytop around 1934. Multiple photographs and newspaper accounts depict the Mount Pocono show as quite large and renowned. Sam Packer promoted Skytop's own show to prepare riders and spectators for the Mount Pocono event and ride the wave of enthusiastic publicity.

Pictured above, Sam Packer awards a loving cup to the winner of the 1932 Ladies Golf Invitational Tourney, Jane McCullough. Fellow participants and committee members stand in the background.

Captured here is a scene from the wood-chopping contest in March 1934. Fox Movietone newsreels filmed some of Skytop's more notorious events, such as the wood-chopping contest and the Pocono Mountain Dogsled Derby. Held in the circle in front of the main lodge, cash rewards drew local competitors. Women even competed, using a buck saw. Aside from this timed two-man sawing, there were single-man axe chopping, veteran's chopping, and champion chopping categories.

Between 1934 and 1940, Skytop hosted the Lackawanna Kennel Club's annual dog show event every August. This show drew between 500 and 600 entries each year. In 1937, event planners added a parade of nations during which the handlers dressed in costumes native to a variety of countries. A local dogs class was held for those wishing to show dogs for the first time, and 55 breeds were represented.

Peck Rake is pictured above with his lead sled dog, Ring. In 1932, Rake won the Pocono Mountain Dog Derby against Buck Hill Falls' musher Harry Drennan. Drennan had become world famous the year before when he transported supplies across the frozen Long Island Sound to Westport, Connecticut, a town cut off by snow. The ensuing fanfare and notoriety bolstered Skytop, Buck Hill, and Pocono Manor to host annual, three-day derbies for nearly a decade before being interrupted, like so much else, by World War II. (Both, courtesy of the Rake family.)

In 1930, Skytop hosted a men's and women's speed-skating competition and invited skate clubs from New York and New Jersey, such as Brooklyn Ice Palace. The speed track oval was constructed on the lower lake, around the ice hockey rink, as shown in the image at left. The photograph below shows the start of the men's race. Both images were taken by Oliver Shannon.

The lower lake in wintertime was the scene of countless ice hockey games whenever the weather allowed. The maintenance involved was no small feat. Amateurs and college clubs competed here as well as the perennial rivalry between Skytop, Buck Hill, and Pocono Manor. A semi-permanent structure was constructed, and lighting was arranged as well. There was enough room for figure skating to go on concurrently with hockey practice. In the photograph above, the structure in the foreground is the bathing house, and behind it and to the left is the first golf house. Both buildings are gone now, and the Lakeview Inn sits in that location. The image below shows a similar scene looking toward the south instead.

A 1941 *New York Times* article announced an ice carnival event at Skytop that featured performances by the Philadelphia Skating Club, the Figure Skating Club of Northern New Jersey, and the Skate Sailing Association of America. Held in January, these skating programs were scheduled in conjunction with house parties and other outdoor winter activities. In the image above, skaters are on the upper lake. The practice ski slope is visible as well as the toboggan run and boathouse. The image below shows skaters on the lower lake and likely predates the photograph above.

This infamous bear lost his life during a January thaw while taking a leisurely stroll across what he thought was a frozen lake. When found, the poor fellow was dragged out and retained to advance Skytop's sportsmen's paradise reputation. Shown here, having been convinced to sit on the bear, are Sam Packer's three children: Lucille in front, Kendric in the middle, and Sam in the back. The retelling of this tale, 80 years hence, still held a note of incredulity and disbelief. (Courtesy of Lucille May and Kendric Packer.)

Sportsmen's weekends were held throughout November and culminated in a December awards ceremony at which, according to a 1936 newsletter, "the great display of the 'Big Kill' hanging in long rows on the South Lawn will put the judges' skill to the keenest test." The bear in the foreground of this photograph may actually have been the one mentioned above. Stories suggest it was temporarily held in cold storage and brought out for photo opportunities.

Skytop's first annual trap shooting tournament was held in 1931. Originally held in front of the lodge, along the second fairway (above), the tournament was also staged along the practice fairway (below). Constructed near the stables, the practice fairway was the result of a tentative change made to accommodate additional cottages. A formal shooting range was later developed up on Skytop Mountain to keep shooting activity away from more populated public space.

Eight

BETTER ON ICE

The caption attached to this early-1930s composition reads, "*Hot Coffee on Ice*: A scene at Skytop Lodge, high in the Pocono Mountains of Pennsylvania, showing some of the guests enjoying invigorating cups of coffee served by Jesse Hollman, the 'skating waiter'. Miss Maude O. Minahan, of New York, secretary to Dean Gildersleeve of Barnard College; Richard Berresford, New York; Mrs. Edward P. O'Reilly, Brooklyn; Miss Jennie Mayer, of Skytop; Arthur Roberts, Merion, PA; and David John Anderson, Skytop." (Courtesy of the Barclay White family.)

This 1938 photograph depicts a tea service on ice, complete with tablecloths, silver sets, cross-country skiers, and the dogsled team. Seated at left and drinking from a cup is Evelyn Myers. The gentleman standing on skis is Frank Shields, and the other gentleman, wearing a dark hat, is J.C. Myers. Others are not identified. Skytop has maintained a tradition of outdoor picnics since before it even opened its doors. Stemming from Sam Packer's habit of leading destination hikes to the vistas and waterfalls of Skytop from Buck Hill Falls Inn, Skytop has habitually hosted lunches, dinners, and afternoon tea in an array of scenic locations around the property. (Courtesy of Eve Myers Doherty.)

A frozen-over lake for Skytoppers of the 1930s and 1940s called for endless amounts of activities. Skate sailing, outdoor dining, skijoring, speed skating, ice hockey, and table tennis are just the start of the list. Skytoppers would never have settled for just simple figure skating. Above, a doubles ping-pong match is played on skates about 1933; below is an undated photograph of a snow plane gliding across the upper lake.

Skate sailing was popular at Skytop in the late 1930s and early 1940s. For this shot, J.C. Myers, son of early investor Jake Myers, sails across Skytop Lake in front of the lodge. J.C. Myers followed in his father's footsteps and became involved in running the lodge and promoting Skytop's myriad activities. He was an avid athlete and skied and skated without hesitation. In the photograph below, his wife, Evelyn, on the other hand, was less of an avid participant. She made frequent publicity appearances nonetheless and amicably provided a lovely smile for this occasion. Both of these images are from the late 1930s.

"Skijoring is a winter sport where a person on skis is pulled by a horse, dog, or motor vehicle and is derived from the Norwegian word ski jøring, meaning ski driving." Shown here behind both a horse and a tractor on Skytop Lake, the popularity of this activity may have been instigated by its appearance as a demonstration sport during the 1928 San Moritz Olympic Games. Alternatively, Sam Packer's unceasing desire to entertain his guests could have serendipitously combined with Skytop's ready supply of skis, ice, rope, and motor power. There are newspaper accounts describing skijoring at Skytop behind an airplane, though no photographs document that event.

In the image above, skijoring has been further modified to include the service of two cows. Sam Packer is second from the right, no doubt the instigator of this idea. Below, another modification employs sleds rather than skis. In this 1938 photograph, girls from the Madeira school had organized a trip to Skytop and were enjoying a tow around Skytop Lake. The Janney house is visible along the shore on the left-hand side of the image, just behind the tractor.

Pictured above is Lucille Packer, wife of Sam Packer, clad in a fuzzy winter hat. With her toes pointed and feet aloft, she seems focused on a safe landing. This artistically captured image appeared in the *New York Tribune*'s rotogravure section publicizing the winter tobogganing craze at Skytop Lodge and elsewhere in the Northeast. Below is a group getting ready to go sledding. The only identified members are Sam Packer, third from the right crouching, and next to him on the sled, his wife, Lucille. (Both, courtesy of Lucille May and Kendric Packer.)

Pictured above are, from left to right, George Tillyou, Bert McCooley, Adelaide Tillyou, Betty McCooley, and Bessie McCooley, about 1929. The very first winter the lodge opened, a tobogganing chute was constructed to accelerate coasting speed and distance. When the lake is frozen, a group of three people might go as fast as 30 miles per hour. Still a popular activity, today's participants wear more protective gear. (Above, courtesy of the Keans family; below, courtesy of Eve Myers Doherty.)

In this series of photographs, playful guests are tempting others to join in the fun, and as usual, Skytop manager Sam Packer, is involved. Ski slopes had not yet been carved out of West Mountain the first few winter seasons the lodge was open. The ski area, illustrated in these two images, was in front of the lodge, over the second fairway, and toward Skytop Lake. The first ski towropes did not appear until 1939, and a Poma lift and warming hut were installed during the 1960s.

Alpine skiing, or downhill skiing, was a new phenomenon in America prior to World War II. Avid skiers thrilled neophytes with their speed and abilities. Skytop instructor Ted Reincke (above) is caught mid-air, while Jack Stokes (at left) made it into the newspapers with this downhill take-off. At this time, skiing attracted a smaller segment of guests than now, and though instructors from Switzerland were hired to teach guests the sport, often there were exhibition-style stunts put on to entertain nonparticipants.

The ski jump shown here predates the towrope and existed from some time in the 1930s through the 1950s. There is no record of its destruction or injury to any person daring enough to use it. It is only known that it was located at the top of the north face of the upper ski slope. Guests would progress from practicing on the second fairway, to the lower slopes, and then the brave would try out the jump. Caricatures of this activity found their way into advertisements and maps well into the 1940s.

Above is a late-1930s image of dedicated skiers inching their way up the slope while simultaneously being distracted by the ski jumpers above them. The elevation change providing Skytop's ski slopes is just enough to warrant the activity and perfect for learning.

Shown here, a cross-country skier or perhaps a downhill skier takes a break in the ice-covered gazebo on top of West Mountain. The small outline of the lodge is visible in the center of the photograph.

The image above captured a frozen-over Indian Ladder Falls in the late 1930s. Evelyn Myers approaches the falls on cross-country skis while her companion uses snowshoes. The notation accompanying the image below cites a severe ice storm in the winter of 1939. Snowshoeing, cross-country skiing, and dog sledding may have shifted to practical necessity rather than pleasant diversion after that storm. (Both, courtesy of Eve Myers Doherty.)

At left, a northern vantage point was used to photograph figure skaters on the lower lake. Unreliable winter temperatures frequently stymied Skytop's ability to offer reliable winter skating. Also, snowy seasons require intensive labor to clear a suitable area. In 1963, a sports pavilion was commissioned to solve these issues. Shown in the photograph below, the pavilion, like the indoor pool constructed a few years earlier, was designed by Peter Paul Muller, the nephew of the lodge's original architect, John Muller.

Nine

SUMMER FUN

Like wintertime, the lower lake was full of activity in summer. The dock and high-diving board live large in the memories of those who learned to swim here. After proving one's skills in the children's area, the next hurdle was that diving board.

The lower lake was the setting for the Camp in the Clouds swim lessons. The stone wall visible in the image at left sectioned off the children's area from deeper area designated for diving adults. This 1933 scene has but one identified student, the youngster on shore, Lucille Packer.

This photograph was taken of Camp in the Clouds girls during one of their regular swimming lessons around 1945. During those years, swim meets were held between Skytop Lodge, Buck Hill Falls Inn, and Pocono Manor. These campers were also taught aquatic ballet. From left to right are unidentified, Sally McCorkle, Sibby Callaway, Holly Sawyer Augenbach, Lynne Derby Graham, Diane ?, Diane Nixon, Bobby Gerstel, and Mary Malleson Briggs. (Courtesy of Lynne Derby Graham.)

116

Although the advent of swimming pools shifted attention away from the lower lake, swimming there had been a profoundly integral part of a summer stay at Skytop. Today, this area has different equipment. Contemporary Skytop guests still experience long hours in the very same place, though today's equipment is inflatable and a rope has replaced the rock wall. Both of these images were taken for publicity around 1934.

In 1960, Peter Muller, nephew of original lodge architect John Muller, was engaged to design an addition to the east wing of the lodge. The natatorium, or indoor pool, was constructed and opened by Christmas 1961; it became a very popular amenity. Shown here are Dupont corporate meeting participants diving off the deep end in 1963. The outdoor pool was added in 1987. (Courtesy of Angelo George.)

The composition at left, likely captured in the late 1930s, was used as inspiration for the mural found inside the natatorium. Painted in 2002 by artist Cora Wooley Waterhouse, the mural was intended to communicate nostalgia for long summer days spent down by the lower lake.

Horseback riding was a regular activity provided at Skytop. The property's vast, undeveloped acreage supplied ample bridle paths for the capable rider. Where the sports pavilion is now was the former site of the riding ring (and before that a baseball field). Lessons were offered to Camp in the Clouds children, and trail rides and occasional overnight trips were led by the riding master. Skytop kept horses and stables, but some years the lodge contracted the work out to a horse farm from Bucks County. In the photograph at right, an unidentified girl poses before one of Skytop's horse shows. In the 1930 image below, an all-female crew poses for the camera. Standing at left is Lucille Packer.

Polo matches were held at Skytop in the late 1930s. Although the image above depicts play on or around the first fairway, other accounts describe the matches being held nearby at the Barrett Airport. Observations written in *Dear Mrs. Bender* describe tall, thin, wobbly players and suggest the necessity of first being a good rider because it spoils the game if one keeps falling off. These images are from a 1937 brochure showing unidentified members of the Skytop team.

Pictured here are the tennis courts before the 1955 flood. After the storm, Skytop relocated the courts to their current location behind the sports pavilion. Har-Tru courts were installed in 1975.

The notation on this mid-1930s image reads, "Trout Anglers Party, Sky Top Lodge, Pa. Left to right, Art Neu, former National Casting Champion, Nathan R. Buller, former State Commissioner of Fisheries (Penna), and Sam H. Packer–'the perfect host'." A fisherman's weekend scheduled in May brought together these men and other members of the Tall Story Club. (Courtesy of Lucille May and Kendric Packer.)

Above all, golf was the most popular activity at Skytop, and everybody played—men, women, and children. Seen here is a young Kendric Packer, proudly displaying his golf swing around 1933.

This photograph of ladies putting on the eighth hole was taken in 1928. The use of short clubs during this era necessitated a stooped posture or sometimes an extremely wide-legged stance. Note the very young caddy. In the background are an old farmhouse (since torn down) and the sloping outline of West Mountain. (Courtesy of the Barclay White family.)

The structure shown here was the first of three buildings on this site. The original Olmsted design called for one large clubhouse with an upper area for a pro shop and a lower area as a bathhouse. Instead, separate buildings were constructed for each function. The one shown here at the 10th tee had a wide observation deck for watching players try to make shots across to the fairway rather than into the lake.

The ladies golf tournament ran annually each July. In this photograph, unidentified committee members pose at the 10th tee. The only known participant is Phyllis Ughetta, far right.

Centered in this late-1930s photograph is four-time governor of New York Alfred E. Smith. Smith tried unsuccessfully to win against Herbert Hoover as the Democratic candidate on the wet ticket in 1928. In 1932, he lost his bid as the Democratic nominee for president to Franklin Roosevelt.

The tall gentleman in the center of photograph is Barclay White. This small golf house structure was in use for caddies and has moved around the property for years. Caddy service officially ended in 1963, not long after the introduction of golf carts. The Caddy Camp was a long-standing institution that proved to be a gateway job for young employees who often stayed on at Skytop for decades.

Shown here as a small boy, Harold Callaway was born in Isle of Wight, England, and grew up playing on the oldest courses in the world. A third generation golfer, his father spent 35 winters in Cannes, on the French Riviera, teaching golf to European nobility. Harold and his brother Lionel came to the United States and influenced the game of golf through long teaching careers of their own and inventions that ranged from special gloves to the Callaway handicap system. Both brothers were golf pros in the Northeast from April to October and golf pros in Pinehurst, North Carolina, from October to April. (Courtesy of the Tufts University Archives.)

Harold Callaway, nicknamed Min by friends due his short stature as well as his incomparable short game, was famed for his perfectly nuanced imitations of just about every club member's golf swing. He first became Skytop's golf pro in 1931.

Harold Callaway poses obligingly for a 1942 piece, drawing ever more promotional attention to Skytop Lodge. This time, rather than attracting participants in competitions to earn silver and gold rewards, Skytop does its part for the war effort and recycles this pile of trophies.

Harold Callaway was a beloved member of the Skytop community. He held the position as head golf pro for 40 summers. His reputation as a teacher attracted hundreds of people from all over the world to come to Skytop for his golf lessons. Perhaps no one was fonder of him than his own daughter, Cybil Callaway, shown here in an embrace with her father about 1955.